JUMBO STICKERS
for **LITTLE HANDS**
Unicorns

Walter Foster Jr.

Jomike Tejido

Quarto.com • WalterFoster.com

© 2021 Quarto Publishing Group USA Inc.

First published in 2021 by Walter Foster Jr., an imprint of The Quarto Group.
100 Cummings Center, Suite 265D, Beverly, MA 01915, USA.
T (978) 282-9590 **F** (978) 283-2742

Walter Foster Jr. titles are also available at discount for retail, wholesale, promotional, and bulk purchase. For details, contact the Special Sales Manager by email at specialsales@quarto.com or by mail at The Quarto Group, Attn: Special Sales Manager, 100 Cummings Center, Suite 265D, Beverly, MA 01915, USA.

ISBN: 978-1-60058-922-5

Illustrations by Jomike Tejido

Printed in China
10 9 8 7 6 5 4 3